As worlds unite

And habitats grow

Find 45 creatures.

Which ones do you know?

This book is dedicated to finding the balance.

Love always to my daughter, Casey Elle,
and special thanks to my friend, Allan Sheather

—K. M. T.

2005 First U.S. edition
Copyright © 2005 by Kim Michelle Toft
All rights reserved, including the right of reproduction in whole or in part in any form.
Charlesbridge and colophon are registered trademarks of Charlesbridge Publishing, Inc.

Published by Charlesbridge
85 Main Street
Watertown, MA 02472
(617) 926-0329
www.charlesbridge.com

First published by the University of Queensland Press, Brisbane, Australia, 2004

Library of Congress Cataloging-in-Publication Data
Toft, Kim Michelle.
  The world that we want/ written and illustrated by Kim Michelle Toft.
     p. cm.
   ISBN 1-58089-114-4 (reinforced for library use)
   ISBN 1-58089-115-2 (softcover)
1. Habitat (Ecology)—Juvenile literature. 2. Rare animals—Juvenile
literature. I. Title
QH541.14T65 2005
577—dc22   2004020717

Printed in China
(hc) 10 9 8 7 6 5 4 3 2 1
(sc) 10 9 8 7 6 5 4 3 2 1

Silk Painting Technique
Each illustration in this book has been hand drawn and painted on silk using a combination of a
latex-based ink called gutta and dyes blended like watercolor. To fix the color, the silk is rolled up
and steamed in a special machine.

Some of the animals in this book are not drawn to scale.

Display type and text type set in 18/42 pt and 12/15 pt Bitstream Amerigo
Color separated, printed, and bound by Everbest Printing Co. Ltd.
Designed by Peter Evans

The World That We Want

Kim Michelle Toft

This is the *air*

that circles the world

that we want.

This is the *rain forest*

that filters the air

that circles the world

that we want.

This is the *river*

that weaves through the forest

that filters the air

that circles the world

that we want.

This is the *mangrove*

that follows the river

that weaves through the forest

that filters the air

that circles the world

that we want.

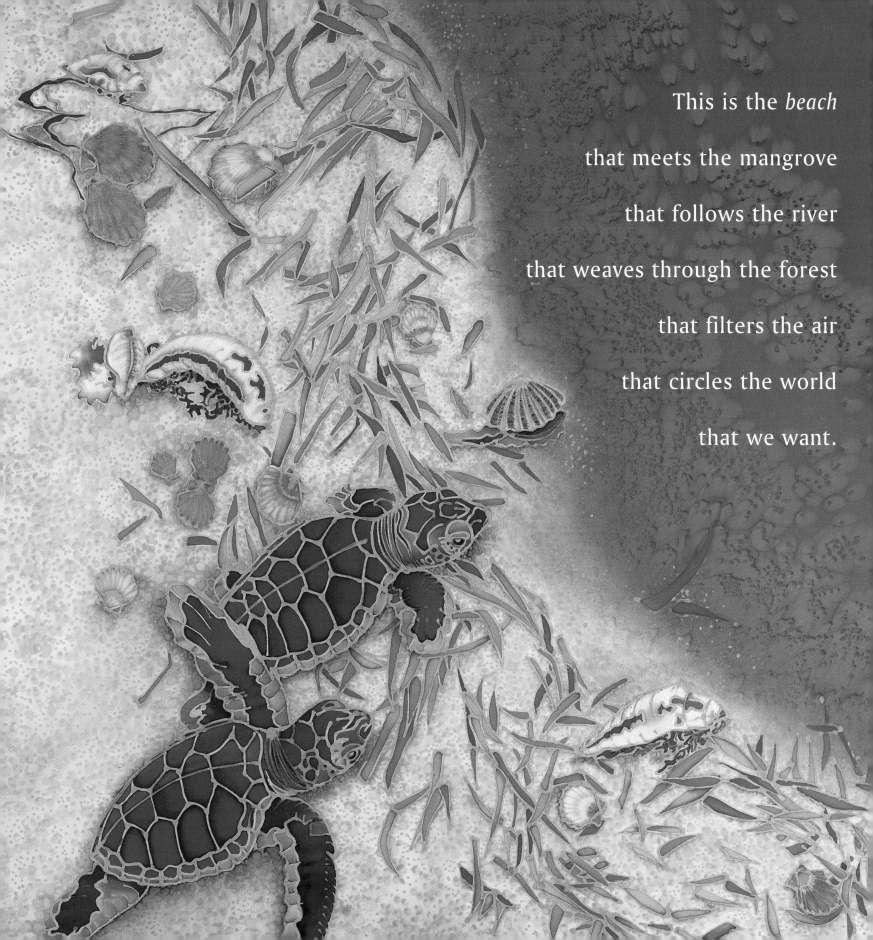

This is the *beach*

that meets the mangrove

that follows the river

that weaves through the forest

that filters the air

that circles the world

that we want.

This is the *tide pool*

that lies on the beach

that meets the mangrove

that follows the river

that weaves through the forest

that filters the air

that circles the world

that we want.

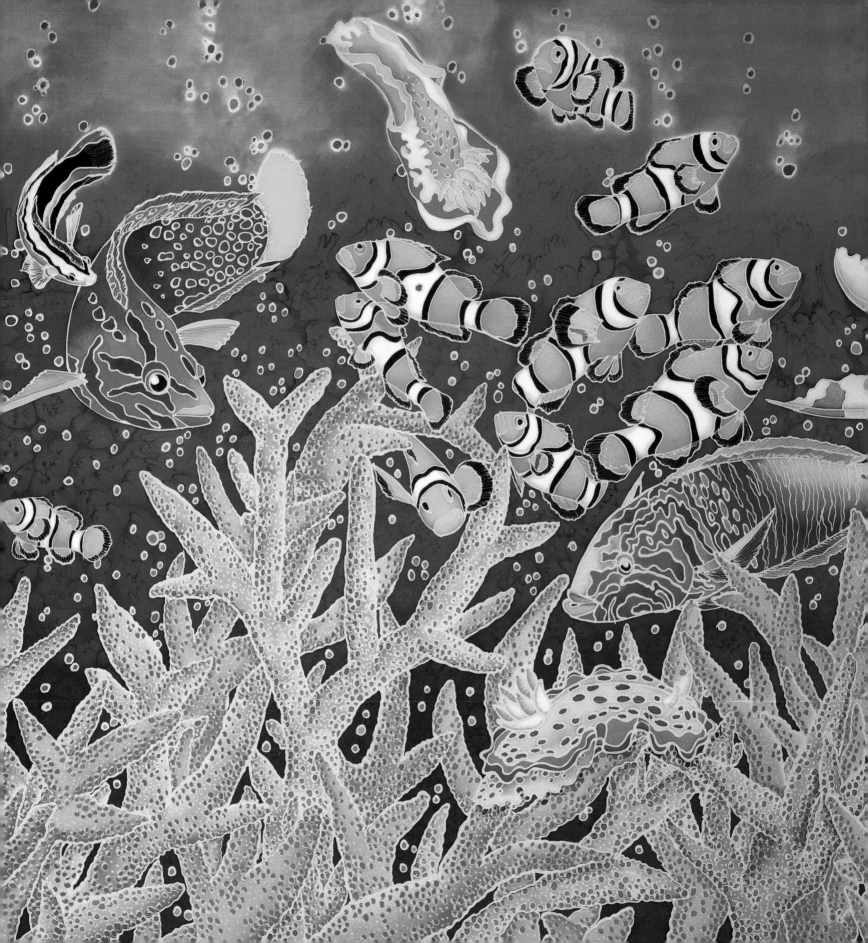

This is the *reef*

that feeds the tide pool

that lies on the beach

that meets the mangrove

that follows the river

that weaves through the forest

that filters the air

that circles the world

that we want.

This is the *atoll*

that grows from the reef

that feeds the tide pool

that lies on the beach

that meets the mangrove

that follows the river

that weaves through the forest

that filters the air

that circles the world

that we want.

The world that we want

The world that we all want and need is one that protects, feeds, and shelters everything that lives in it. The biggest threat to wildlife communities today is the destruction of their habitats. Many of the habitats in this book are threatened by pollution, deforestation, or climatic changes. If these habitats are destroyed then each one of the species that lives there is put at risk. All living things need to be kept in balance if we are to keep the world that we want.

AIR

Air is a mixture of invisible gases that makes up Earth's atmosphere. When large amounts of industrial fumes or smoke escape into the air, they cause pollution and smog, which poisons animals and plants in the area.

1. RED-TAILED TROPIC BIRDS soar over the ocean, stopping on oceanic islands to breed. In the breeding season their long tail looks like two bright red ribbons.
2. RED-FOOTED BOOBIES are large seabirds that are found in tropical waters, diving for fish and squid. Although boobies can be found far out at sea, more often they stay near their nest in trees or shrubs.
3. FRIGATE BIRDS, with their eight-foot wingspan, fly over tropical seas for long periods of time, landing only to sleep or breed. They are known for their flying skills, which allow them to catch food easily or to snatch food from other birds.
4. SEA EAGLES are the second largest bird of prey in Australia, measuring almost three feet from head to tail. They are found near rivers, lakes, bays, and islands.
5. Of the eight species of PELICANS found around the world, Australian pelicans are the largest. They can remain in flight up to 24 hours. They live and breed in colonies near water.

RAIN FOREST

Rain forests are tropical woodlands that receive about 100 inches of rain per year. Deforestation, the clearing of rain forests, endangers the wide variety of plant and animal life here.

6. CASSOWARIES are large, flightless birds that measure up to six feet tall. Cassowaries eat fruit, much of which passes whole through their digestive system. The undigested fruit takes root to create trees throughout the rain forest.
7. SPOTTED CUSCUS are marsupials, meaning the females have a pouch to carry their young. They sleep most of the day, and move slowly through the upper canopy of the rain forest at night, searching for fruit and leaves to eat.
8. ULYSSES BUTTERFLIES live high up in the rain forest canopy. These brilliantly colored butterflies come down to ground level to find food.
9. GREEN PYTHONS are not poisonous snakes, but they do have long teeth that can give a nasty bite. They are reptiles, meaning they are cold-blooded and their young hatch from eggs. Green pythons sleep during the day and hunt for birds, frogs, lizards, and small mammals at night.
10. RED-EYED TREE FROGS live in trees and come down to the ground to breed. They are amphibians, meaning they live in water when they are young and live on land as adults. Red-eyed tree frogs feed mainly at night on insects.

This is the *ocean*

that shapes the atoll

that grows from the reef

that feeds the tide pool

that lies on the beach

that meets the mangrove

that follows the river

that weaves through the forest

that filters the air

that circles the world

that we want.

RIVER

Rivers are large streams. Water provides support for plant and animal life around the river. Nutrients in the water also provide food for some animals. Pollutants, such as chemicals and waste, can destroy river life.

11. RAINBOW FISH are small, the longest measuring three inches. They are colorful fish, usually marked with stripes or colored scales.

12. SAW-SHELL TURTLES are reptiles, and they live in slow-moving freshwater rivers, swamps, and lakes. They feed on fruit, crayfish, snails, and fish.

13. LITTLE KINGFISHERS are about five inches long and have a short tail and a long beak. They live near small rivers, catching fish or crayfish for food.

14. WATER DRAGONS are large lizards that measure up to three feet from their head to the end of their long tail. They run fast and are also strong swimmers. These reptiles feed mainly on insects.

15. CRAYFISH are crustaceans, meaning they have hard shells and antennae. They can move across land and swim through water. They live in burrows, coming out to eat plants, insects, and fish.

MANGROVE

Mangrove trees can live in salt water, and they grow on the edge of rivers close to the sea. They provide shelter and food for crabs, fish, and birds. Chemical spills can wipe out this ecosystem.

16. STRIPED BUTTERFISH feed on small animals and plants found on the riverbed. The spines on their fins are poisonous.

17. ROYAL SPOONBILLS catch small fish, shellfish, and frogs to eat. As they wade through the water, spoonbills sweep their bill from side to side to scoop up their food.

18. FIDDLER CRABS are crustaceans, and they live in estuaries, the part of a river where it meets the ocean. Male fiddler crabs have one claw larger than the other, which they wave to warn other crabs away or to attract a mate.

19. SALTWATER CROCODILES are the largest living reptiles, measuring up to 23 feet long. They can live to be 100 years old. They eat turtles, snakes, birds, crabs, and small mammals.

20. MUDSKIPPERS can live both in water and on land. They use their fins as legs to skip over the mud, returning to the water to keep their body moist. They feed on insects.

BEACH

Beaches are created over millions of years by waves grinding against rocks and shells and breaking them down into fine particles. Pollution and beach erosion—caused by storms and global warming—are some of the dangers facing this environment.

21. SILVER GULLS are shore birds. These scavengers will eat just about anything left over by humans as well as insects, crustaceans, and fish.

22. Female GREEN SEA TURTLES lay their eggs on the beach. After hatching, the tiny baby turtles rush to the ocean, but many of them are eaten by gulls or crabs before they reach the water.

23. SCALLOPS are mollusks, soft-bodied animals usually protected by a hard shell. Scallops have two shells that are hinged together. They move by clapping their shells.

24. The PORTUGUESE MAN-OF-WAR looks like a jellyfish but is really made up of four different kinds of tiny animals. Its tentacles can give a nasty sting.

25. GHOST CRABS live in burrows in sand dunes and come out at night to look for food. These crustaceans make a loud creaking noise.

TIDE POOL

Tide pools are rocky areas between the land and the ocean that are filled with seawater. This shelter for smaller creatures is affected by changes in the sun, wind, and water.

26. BLUE-RINGED OCTOPUSES are small but deadly. Their blue rings are only visible when they're about to attack. These mollusks eat mainly shrimp and small crabs.

27. SEA ANEMONES are invertebrates, meaning they have no backbone. Their mouth is surrounded by tentacles that catch food, such as fish, mussels, and worms. Anemones use a sucker disc to attach themselves to rocks.

28. MUSSELS are found all around the world. These mollusks have two dark, hinged shells.

29. SEA STARS are shaped like stars with a mouth in the center and five or more arms spreading out from the middle. They eat mollusks, crabs, and fish.

30. BLENNIES are small fish with slimy skin rather than scales. They live in crevices of coral or tide pools, where they feed on plants such as algae.

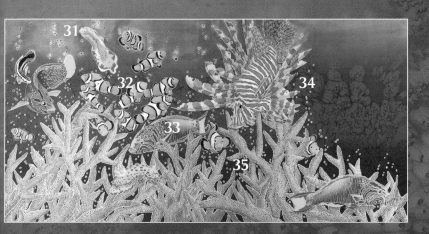

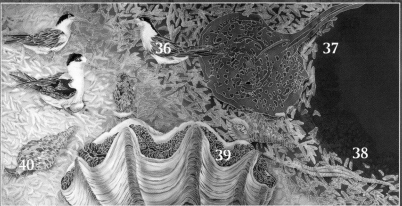

REEF

Coral reefs are the most biologically diverse environments on earth. Reefs around the world are under threat from pollution and changing climatic conditions.

31. NUDIBRANCH SEA SLUGS are like snails without a shell. They feed on soft corals.
32. CLOWNFISH are the only fish able to live in the stinging tentacles of sea anemones without being stung. In return for this protection, clownfish clean the anemones.
33. WRASSE are long fish that feed on shellfish during the daytime. At night they either bury themselves in sand or wedge themselves into crevices in the reef.
34. LIONFISH have long, poisonous dorsal spines. They hide during the day and come out at night to feed on small fish and crustaceans.
35. STAGHORN CORAL is a hard coral. The polyps of this coral lay down a bony skeleton that helps build the reef and provides protection.

ATOLL

Atolls are coral islands made up of a reef that surrounds a lagoon. They suffer from the same threats as reefs do.

36. BLACK CRESTED TERNS are found on coral islands and in sheltered areas on the coast. They eat fish, mollusks, crustaceans, and insects.
37. BLUE-SPOTTED STINGRAYS are wide, flat, kite-shaped fish with a long whip-like tail that has poisonous spines on it. They often bury themselves in the sand on the ocean floor, looking for crabs and shrimp.
38. PIPEFISH are related to seahorses. Male pipefish have a pouch in their belly where they carry their young. Pipefish eat crustaceans.
39. GIANT CLAMS are among the largest shelled animals, measuring up to four feet long. During the day they lie on a reef with their shells open and their body hanging over the edge.
40. TRUMPET SHELLS are among the largest living snails and can grow up to 20 inches in length. They are one of the few marine animals that feed on the coral-eating crown-of-thorns sea star.

OCEAN

Oceans are bodies of saltwater that cover 70 percent of Earth's surface. Water from the ocean evaporates into the atmosphere and then falls back to the earth in the form of rain. Oil spills, trash, and other pollutants can have a negative effect on the ocean itself and the life it supports.

41. HUMPBACK WHALES are mammals, meaning they are warm-blooded and have a backbone. They migrate between their breeding and feeding grounds each year. They feed in tropical areas, eating fish and krill.

42. BOTTLENOSE DOLPHINS are mammals and are related to whales. They eat fish and squid, finding their prey by echolocation, a method of bouncing sound waves off of objects.

43. BARRACUDA are large, measuring about three feet. They are fierce fish that often move in packs around reef slopes, chasing and eating other fish.

44. MARLIN can grow up to 14 feet long and weigh over 1,500 pounds. They are very fast, strong fish that are often hunted for sport.

45. HAMMERHEAD SHARKS have a great sense of smell, which helps them find fish, stingrays, and octopus. Sometimes they use their "hammer" to hold down their prey.